QUIT THAT TEMPER

A Complete Guide to understanding Anger and Managing it

Dr Jason Keller

Quit That Temper: A complete guide to understanding anger and managing it by Dr. Jason Keller

CHAPTER 1

Quit That Temper

Temper may also refer to a propensity to lose control when furious. Ask your pals if you're unsure whether you have a temper; just don't get upset if you don't like what they say.

Temper has several overlapping yet different meanings. Temperament can relate to a person's general mood as well as their propensity to get upset; in this case, you would use the terms "angry" or "gentle" to characterize someone's temper. Additionally, the word temper can indicate "to constrain." Counting to ten anytime you feel the want to have a "temper tantrum" or fit will help you control your temper if you have a bad one.

Anger will be our primary theme in this literary piece.

What is Anger?

Anger is a feeling that is defined by hostility toward someone or something that you believe has intentionally wronged you.

How we respond to an angry situation is influenced by three different forms of aggression. These include Assertive Anger, Open Aggression, and Passive Aggression. Assertive Anger is the finest strategy when you're furious. Check out what each sort of big word implies.

- Passive Aggression

Because they don't want confrontation, many people find it difficult to confess when they are furious. This is known as passive aggression. This manifests itself in behaviors such as pouting, procrastinating (putting off tasks that need to be completed), and pretending "everything is OK." A need to maintain control underlies passive aggressiveness. Do you need help with it? Read on to learn more about "assertive fury."

- Open Aggression

On the other side, many people tend to act violently or verbally out of fury, which frequently results in harm to oneself or others. The term for this is open aggression. Fighting, bullying, blackmailing, accusing, yelling, quarreling, sarcasm, and criticism are ways in which this manifests itself. Open hostility results from a need for control. Do you need assistance with overt aggression? Read on to learn more about "assertive fury." See the section on self-harm for further information on how anger can occasionally be vented on things or even on oneself.

- Assertive Anger

Being calm and self-assured, communicating and listening, and being receptive to assistance in handling the issue are all good ways to cope with rage. Relationships can develop as a result of this assertive fury. It entails planning your words before you utter them, being certain in your delivery, yet remaining receptive and adaptable to the "other side." It entails exercising patience, keeping your voice down, expressing your emotional state, and making an effort to comprehend how others are experiencing. Assertively managing your anger shows maturity and concern for your relationships and personal well-being.

Always be willing to forgive if someone has shown regret for having upset you or if you have come to the conclusion that the issue "isn't worth it." Be ready to forgive others as well as yourself! You'll feel better after doing this, and your interpersonal interactions will improve.

Anger has its benefits. For instance, it may provide you with a means of expressing unfavorable emotions or inspire you to seek answers to issues.

However, uncontrolled anger might lead to issues. Anger impairs your physical and mental health because it raises blood pressure and causes other bodily changes that impair your ability to think clearly.

CHAPTER 2

How to Identify and deal with Anger

Anger is an unpleasant emotional state that is frequently accompanied by antagonistic thoughts, physical arousal, and unhelpful activities.

How to identify and manage anger

Everyone is familiar with how anger feels. However, it is not always clear what anger is, what it does, or how to regulate it. Psychologists can assist individuals in identifying and avoiding rage triggers. They may also offer advice on how to handle anger when it does arise.

The following inquiries regarding anger are answered by Howard Kassinove, Ph.D., a psychologist who specializes in anger:

How does anger vary from aggressiveness, and what does it mean?

Anger is an unpleasant emotional state that is frequently accompanied by antagonistic thoughts, physical arousal, and unhelpful activities. It typically arises in response to another person's unfavorable behaviors that are seen as being disrespectful, belittling, threatening, or careless. Certain ways of thinking, such as "My supervisor chastised me in front of my coworkers," are associated with anger. I'm now furious. He shouldn't treat people that poorly! or "That woman is driving so slowly in front of me. Exasperating, this. She shouldn't be permitted to operate a vehicle on a motorway! Anger fuels our desire to take action. According to our statistics, roughly 25% of angry outbursts contain plans for retaliation, such as "I'm going to spread stories about my employer to get even" or "I'd like to just bump her car to put her in her place." It's interesting to note that encounters with individuals we like or love, such as children, spouses, and close friends, often result in rage.

Muscle tension, headaches, or an elevated heart rate might be symptoms of angry thoughts. Additionally, the verbal and physical signs of anger may be used to alert others to our irritation. Yelling, arguing, swearing, and sarcasm are some of the verbal expressions. The act of slamming a wall, tossing a book to the ground, breaking a pencil, or raising a clenched fist are all examples of physical ways to communicate anger. Anger can occasionally be internalized rather than displayed externally.

Contrarily, aggression is defined as deliberate action intended to cause harm to another person. It frequently shows a desire for power and authority. Weapons are frequently used in the instances I observe in my clinical and research work. In addition to marital violence, child or elder abuse, bullying, gang, and criminal activity, aggression can be demonstrated by punching, shoving, striking, or even maiming another person.

Since loud verbalizations are the only way that rage is normally communicated, cases of aggressiveness are the ones that end up in the criminal justice system. According to our research, 90 percent of violent situations begin with rage. Aggression, however, only follows 10% of rage feelings. Fortunately, the majority of people do not act aggressively when they are furious, despite their want to do so. Additionally, while irritated, there is occasionally a tendency to act in problem-solving ways.

However, anger is a significant issue in and of itself, with detrimental effects on many facets of life, including relationships, the job, parent-child interactions, and driving behavior. Interpersonal disputes, poor opinions from others, erratic driving, property destruction, poor job adaptability, taking improper risks, accidents, substance addiction, and so-called crimes of passion are all linked to anger.

What are a few of the benefits of anger?

Anger has many detrimental long-term effects. However, rage has a biological origin. The fight-or-flight response includes it. In the past, it served as a means of survival, and it still has certain advantages now. However, many of these are just long-term advantages because few of us enjoy being around angry people.

A legitimate response to injustice may be anger. The social movements for equality for people of color, the elderly, and women, among others, undoubtedly benefited from rage. Additionally, anger may improve the results of business discussions and raise our desire to make the world a better place.

One benefit is its alerting capability. Anger signals to people that we need their attention, that we are disturbed, and that it is best to be mindful of our words and actions. It could also result in other people complying. At a retail counter, insisting that we were first in line would result in better treatment. Additionally, when we are furious, children and other people can be more willing to comply with our requests in the short term. When said forcefully to a young child, "Don't go in the street without clutching mommy's hand!" can save their lives.

Sometimes feeling angry just feels justified and nice. When we see a play or a movie where a character suffers unjustly, we could become incensed. Eventually, anger is replaced with a sense of contentment as virtue prevails over evil. Playwrights have been aware of this for centuries. Similar to this, rage gives people a particular passion for life. Can you picture a world without resentment? We all seem to like the spice that milder, healthier levels of anger and aggravation provide to our daily lives.

What are some possible negative effects of anger on one's health?

Many individuals believe that having too much anger is only a psychological issue. That's a glaring oversimplification. The autonomic nervous system is activated when we get furious. For instance, the sympathetic nervous system will likely be aroused in response to the discovery of a spouse's covert affair, which would likely result in corresponding hormonal and neurochemical alterations. Increases in cardiovascular response, respiration, sweat, the blood supply to working muscles, and strength can all result from these physiological processes. Many bodily systems, including the cardiovascular, immunological, digestive, and central neurological systems, will be impacted while the rage lasts. This may result in delayed wound healing and a probable rise in the risk of certain malignancies, as well as higher risks of hypertension, stroke, heart disease, stomach ulcers, and bowel illnesses.

Anger is a recognized independent risk factor for heart disease, according to research. High trait anger is the propensity to become angry often and in many contexts. One study tracked 12,986 persons for almost three years and discovered that those with the normal blood pressure but a high characteristic of anger had a two to three times higher risk of coronary events. Another investigation tracked 4,083 people for ten to fifteen years. The risk of fatal and nonfatal cardiovascular events was highest in those with the lowest levels of anger management. Following a study of the literature, specialists have concluded that persistent hostility, acute anger episodes, and high levels of rage are all risk factors for cardiovascular disease. Anger that is experienced seldom, intensely, and persistently may be less destructive than anger that is experienced mildly and expressed assertively.

Why are some people more prone to rage than others, according to psychological research?

Examining a person's propensity for anger requires looking at their thoughts, bodily responses, and physical behavior. When it comes to physiological responses, some people are readily stimulated and react swiftly to unpleasant stimuli. They quickly become enraged by unpleasant odors, heat, and loud noises. Others take their time to respond and don't appear affected by such stimuli. Here, genetic variability is important.

Sulking, slamming on the desk, and punching the wall are examples of physical displays of rage that people acquire through imitating others and receiving rewards.

Last but not least, some data shows that playing violent video games and maybe listening to furious music with violent lyrics may exacerbate anger and violence in certain people. The soundtrack in violent video games is fast-paced and agitated. They acquire the skills of hypervigilance, impulsive action, and enemy killing. This results in reinforcement in the form of points, the purchase of additional weapons, entry into more difficult game levels, and praise from other players in the gaming area.

What are some actions people may take to cope with rage among friends or family members? What would make them different from interacting with a stranger, like a store clerk, cab driver, or other service providers?

The rage experienced while interacting with strangers results from brief encounters. The cashier, the driver, or the waiter might not ever appear again. You often answer "not very significant at all" when you assess the importance of a bothersome circumstance. The worst that has happened to you is that you may have overpaid for the cab or the cashier may have delayed you by a few minutes. Work around these unpleasant circumstances by realizing that they are not emergencies. To return a purchase, choose a different restaurant or visit the store after closing time.

Recognize the distinction between circumstances you have control over and those that are out of your control. Inform the cab driver of your intended route before you get in. Before the server disappears from the table and is never seen again after you order that steak at the restaurant, request more ketchup. Other occurrences are beyond your control. For a variety of reasons, flights regularly arrive late. You have limited options. Accept the wait as a chance to read or unwind rather than something terrible or deserving of rage.

Because of the continual encounters, the rage experienced when interacting with family or friends is distinct. The quickest and simplest self-help techniques for dealing with this type of rage include avoidance and flight, relaxation, cognitive restructuring, and aggressive expression.

It might not be wise to tackle every issue head-on. Sometimes it's best to stay away from a situation that might get heated. Allow your spouse, for instance, to handle a rude store clerk or an unruly child. Learn to periodically rely on others to help you solve challenges. Since people who are furious tighten their muscles and experience headaches and stomachaches, relaxation is an excellent strategy for managing anger. Locate a peaceful place and a chair that is supportive of the arms and legs. Focus on letting the muscles naturally relax while taking deep breaths. Recognize that learning to relax your muscles requires practice. Oftentimes, soothing music is beneficial. Cognitive restructuring is the process of developing the ability to properly assess unpleasant circumstances. Experiences of anger are frequently accompanied by cognitive distortions, such as false perceptions of the significance of the incident or of one's ability to deal. Anger is a moral feeling that is frequently connected to "should"-style demands for justice. Adults who are upset also tend to overgeneralize the implications of other people's actions and to think in "either/or" scenarios, such as "Either he's my buddy or he's not." That's all there is to it! Learn to view difficult circumstances not just as terrible but also as an opportunity to gain coping mechanisms and adopt new behaviors. Accept that people may do both good and negative things. Stop making such sweeping assumptions about individuals.

Being assertive entails expressing anger in a straightforward, acceptable, and non-demeaning manner. It is OK to state, "When you declared my work was mediocre in front of the others, I felt irritated," if you had been insulted or treated disrespectfully. I want to discuss the problem with you so that we can strengthen our bond. To remark, "You acted like a terrible jerk today," is quite another. You have no right to speak that way in front of the group! You too have a lot of issues!

When should someone who is angry seek professional assistance?

We will all experience rage at some point in our life. So, the key query is: "Is my anger serving me well?" Professional assistance is not required when anger is small, rare, passes quickly, and is addressed assertively (straight to the problematic individual, in a non-accusatory way) and without aggressiveness.

In certain situations, anger may only serve to make you more irritated and may even help solve the issue.

However, there is cause for concern if your anger is moderate to severe, frequent, lasts to the point where you are harboring resentment and plotting revenge, and is displayed through violent verbal and physical behaviors. Inappropriate rage expression may put you in danger of a bad relationship, health issues, and even legal consequences.

What are the best interventions for those who struggle with severe anger issues and want to master their emotions?

Anger control is effective. Adult anger management programs have been the subject of six in-depth evaluations. The most recent one included 96 trials and found that psychological therapies are modestly helpful for managing anger in a range of populations. This includes initiatives to lessen rage in medical settings, community treatment centers, prisons, and colleges and universities. In other cases, significant improvements may be seen after as little as eight therapy sessions, and the effects persisted during follow-ups lasting anywhere from a month to a year. The most effective treatment plans use many components. The most effective interventions are those based on psychodynamic therapy, cognitive or cognitive-behavioral therapy, and skill development. Programs for relaxation, stress prevention, and exposure-based therapies are also beneficial.

It is advisable for those looking for anger management services to start with their local hospitals or colleges and to enquire about how long they have been providing such services. The finest service is probably provided by staff who are knowledgeable about the most recent research, have received specialized training, and have greater expertise in the field of anger management.

CHAPTER 3

Anger and Personal Health

Long-term medical consequences of unchecked rage include heightened anxiety, elevated blood pressure, and headaches.

If used wisely, anger may be a healthy and productive emotion.

Regular exercise, mastering relaxation skills, and therapy are long-term anger control solutions.

Anger that is well controlled may be a motivating feeling for you to change for the better. On the other hand, rage is a strong feeling that, if not controlled, may be harmful to both you and others who are close to you. Arguments, physical altercations, physical abuse, assault, and self-harm can result from unchecked fury.

Anger's physical repercussions

Anger sets off the body's "fight or reaction" mechanism. This reaction is also influenced by other emotions including fear, enthusiasm, and anxiety. Adrenaline and cortisol, two stress chemicals, are abundant in the body thanks to the adrenal glands. In advance of physical effort, the brain diverts blood away from the intestines and into the muscles. The body temperature rises, the heart rate, blood pressure, and breathing quicken, and the skin begins to perspire. The brain is concentrated and honed.

Health issues including rage

Chronic unchecked rage can eventually affect a variety of bodily systems due to the persistent influx of stress hormones and related metabolic changes.

Uncontrolled rage has been related to both short- and long-term health issues, including:

headache, digestive issues, including stomach discomfort, increased anxiety, and depression

heart attack, stroke, and skin conditions like eczema due to high blood pressure.

Managing your rage in constructive ways

Here are some tips on how to deal with your rage constructively

1. Take a little break from the situation if you feel out of control so you can calm down.
2. Accept that feelings are common and a natural aspect of life.
3. Try to identify the precise causes of your anger.
4. Consider devising several plans of action to address the issue once you have determined what it I
5. s.Exercise your body by playing sports or going for a run.
6. Discuss your feelings with a trusted person.

Unproductive methods for managing anger

Many people use damaging and improper methods to vent their anger, such as:

Explosions of wrath: Some people have a very difficult time controlling their emotions and frequently erupt in rages. Physical abuse or violent behavior can result from raging anger. When someone can't manage their rage, they may become distant from friends and family. Some people who get angry easily lack self-confidence and use their anger to control others and make themselves feel strong. Visit the White Ribbon Australia website's page on "What is violence against women?" for more information.

Repressing anger is a choice made by certain people who believe that anger is an unsuitable or "evil" feeling. However, suppressed rage frequently manifests as worry and sadness. Some people choose to let out their pent-up rage on helpless individuals like kids or animals.

Managing disagreements

It is simple to continue being angry or unhappy with the other person after an argument. A fight with someone you see frequently might be quite uncomfortable if you don't find a solution.

It could or might not be helpful to discuss your dispute with the individual. If you do speak with them, make sure it is in a constructive manner. Maintain your composure and speak honestly and frankly.

It can be preferable to avoid direct contact with them if they have a history of violence or abuse. If you feel secure doing so and if they are receptive to seeking a resolution to the conflict, you might speak with them on the phone. Asking someone to accompany you and encourage you when you make the contact later may be beneficial.

Instead of attempting to tell them how you feel, try to express how you feel as a result of their viewpoint. You can agree to disagree. You might want more assistance to settle the dispute. You might request a reliable third party to act as a mediator so you two can hear the other side of the story.

Argument management strategies

There are several justifications for handling conflicts, including:

You'll feel more accomplished and upbeat as a result of it.

You could see improvements in your ability to unwind, stay healthy, and sleep well.

You could create more solid bonds with others.

You could sense happiness.

Advice for long-term anger control

It can take some time for you to change the way you usually express your anger. Keep a journal of your angry outbursts to attempt to figure out how and why you become angry.

Think about taking an assertiveness course or getting some conflict resolution training.

Study calming methods like yoga or meditation.

If you are still upset over prior occurrences, go to a counselor or psychologist.

Regular exercise

the advantages of routine exercise for mood control

Anger is more likely to occur in those under stress. Regular exercise has been shown in several studies to boost mood and lower stress levels. This may be because physical activity helps to burn off stress hormones and increases the brain's synthesis of neurotransmitters and moods that control moods, such as endorphins and catecholamines.

Teaching young people how to be angry

Adequately expressing rage is a taught trait. The following ideas can help your kid manage intense emotions:

Set a good example.

Inform children that anger is normal and should be expressed healthily.

Respect your child's feelings at all times.

instilling useful problem-solving abilities.

Encourage candid and open dialogue at home.

Permit them to vent their rage healthily.

Describe the differences between rage and aggressiveness.

Have repercussions for violence or aggressive behavior, but not for inappropriately expressed anger.

Teach your child many techniques for self-soothing and relaxation.

CHAPTER 4

How to control anger

Manage your anger before it manages you.

Anger is an entirely typical and typically positive human emotion. But it can cause issues if it spirals out of control and becomes destructive.

Psychologists can assist individuals in identifying and avoiding the situations that make them furious. They can also offer advice on how to control the unavoidable rage that occasionally erupts without notice.

How to Handle Anger

A psychologist offers the following advice on using emotional intelligence to control your anger:1. An easy experiment demonstrates the connection between your ideas and your furious feelings.

Do you ever become truly furious? And what happens when it does, particularly at work, and what are the results—good or bad? I'm not referring to the competitive fervor you could get after a rival outsells you in a lucrative transaction and you feel compelled to outdo them the next time. When someone treats you unfairly, insults you, or even cuts you off in traffic, anger may become overwhelming.

That type of rage might make you feel powerless, worthless, sorry for yourself, and unable to concentrate on your current activities. Wouldn't it be wonderful if you could somehow control your anger when it first surfaces, allowing you to make rational decisions about how to react? There is a solution, though, and it comes from understanding the reality of fury. Although it is an emotion, it is a direct outcome of your thoughts and the significance you attribute to the words or actions that have offended you.

Jeffrey Nevid, Ph.D., a psychologist, suggests a straightforward experiment to demonstrate it: Make yourself angry for 60 seconds while your mind is entirely blank. Yes, you may quickly conjure up that horrible thing your spouse said or the way your boss never provides you with the information you want and feel blazingly angry. But attempt to feel it without contemplating anything. Nevid claims that if you're like the majority of people, you can't truly do it.

That implies, in his writing, that ideas are always the cause of our wrath. The problem is that those ideas could be wholly erroneous. I once had mournful wrath when I was approximately 10 years old when, after a disagreement, my mother referred to me as a "sickening kid." That's what I overheard, at least. Later, I learned that she had stated, "I'm sick and exhausted."

Of course, not all angry outbursts are the consequence of hearing something someone else stated incorrectly. But it frequently results from interpreting and comprehending someone else's actions and statements rather than attempting to understand their thoughts and feelings. Nevid also provides a one-minute practice for controlling your rage and restoring your composure in light of this.

As is the case with many emotions that we attempt to suppress or dismiss, trying to convince yourself that you are not furious when you are won't help you get over your anger; instead, it will just make it greater. Don't dismiss it or dispute it, then. Admit your anger to yourself, and if appropriate, don't hold it in from other people as well.

Have you ever noticed that anytime we become enraged, we see it as having been done to us? We claim that other people and things "make" us furious, making us seem like helpless victims of that feeling. Bruce Banner, who begs, "Don't make me furious," serves as an example of this because if you do, against his will, he will turn into the Incredible Hulk.

I don't intend to imply that you choose to become angry. Usually, something does kick it off.

However, as Nevid's experiment of 60 seconds demonstrates, rage cannot survive apart from your thoughts about whatever it was that gave you that feeling. Therefore, the story you tell yourself about what triggered your anger can either fuel it more or cause it to simmer down. You are in control.

How to manage your rage: Keeping your rage under control

Anger is a normal human emotion, and there are occasionally good reasons to be angry. However, unchecked rage may be detrimental to your relationships and health. Thankfully, there are strategies you may learn to help you control your anger.

The capacity to comprehend, control, and affect one's own emotions, as well as those of others, is known as emotional intelligence, or EQ. To understand and accept your feelings as well as to comprehend and sympathize with others, you must have emotional intelligence (EQ). You never know why the person who just cut you off in traffic is rushing to the hospital—possibly because a loved one is sick. It's possible that the coworker who just called you names didn't mean to disrespect you. Or, perhaps he or she is simply having a terrible day and is behaving out as a result. Or you may be taking offense to something that wasn't intended for you.

The impulse to respond to improper anger with your fury is stifled, according to Nevid, when you approach the other person with empathy (precise knowledge of the other person's sentiments). If you can accomplish that, you can prevent a dispute from becoming out of hand. You could learn more about the folks that irritate you. They could even comprehend you more fully.

Ten suggestions for controlling your anger

Controlling your anger might be difficult. Take a timeout or use "I" words as part of your easy anger management strategies to maintain control.

When someone cuts you off in traffic, do you become angry? When your child refuses to comply, does your blood pressure spike? It's normal and even good to feel angry. However, it's crucial to approach it constructively. Uncontrolled rage may harm your relationships and your health.

Are you ready to regulate your anger? Start by taking into account these 10 anger control suggestions.

1. Be thoughtful before you talk

It's simple to say something you'll later regret when you're under the influence of emotion. Before you speak, take a minute to gather your thoughts. Permit those who are involved in the issue to do the same as well.

2. When you're at ease, voice your worries.

When you're able to speak clearly, be forceful yet non-aggressive when you vent your dissatisfaction. Clearly and simply express your demands and concerns without inflicting harm or attempting to exert control over others.

3. Take a workout.

Exercise can assist in lowering the tension that might make you furious. If you see that your wrath is growing, take a quick stroll or run. Or spend some time engaging in some other fun physical activity.

4. Take a break.

Not just timeouts for children. During difficult moments of the day, allow yourself brief pauses. You could feel more equipped to manage what is ahead without becoming upset or furious if you have a few quiet moments to yourself.

5. List potential answers

Work on fixing the problem at hand rather than dwelling on the thing that enraged you. Are you upset about your child's filthy room? Knock on the door. Every night, does your partner arrive late for dinner? Plan your meals for later in the day. Or decide to eat alone a couple of times per week. Additionally, be aware that some circumstances are just beyond your control. Regarding what you can and cannot alter, try to be practical. Remind yourself that becoming angry won't help and can even make things worse.

6. Constantly use "I" phrases

Criticizing or blaming others could only make things tenser. Instead, characterize the issue using "I" sentences. Be considerate and specific. Instead of saying, "You never do any housekeeping," try saying, "I'm disappointed that you left the table without offering to assist with the dishes."

7. Don't harbor resentment

It is a strong instrument to forgive. You risk becoming overcome by bitterness or a sense of unfairness if you let anger and other negative emotions overpower happy ones. If you forgive the person who offended you, your relationship may improve and you both may be able to benefit from the experience.

8. Laugh to relieve anxiety

Laughter can assist reduce tension. Use humor to help you confront the things that are upsetting you and, maybe, any irrational expectations you may have about how things should turn out. Though it might hurt sentiments and worsen situations, avoid using sarcasm.

9. Work on relaxing techniques

Use your relaxation techniques when your anger starts to flare. Try deep breathing exercises, visualize a soothing environment, or repeat a word or phrase that is comforting, such as "Take it easy." To promote relaxation, you might also do some yoga positions, write in a notebook, or listen to music.

10. Know when to ask for assistance

It might be difficult to learn how to manage your anger at times. If your anger appears out of control, makes you do things you regret, or harms people around you, get therapy for anger issues.

DESSERT

In the words of the great Aristotle, “Anybody can become angry- that is easy, but to be angry with the right person and to the right degree and at the right time and for the right purpose, and in the right way- that is not within everybody's power and is not easy."

Anger would always have it's positives and negatives but one who regulates or has a hold on his temper, will go quite far.

In case you're in need of some guidance, you can reach out to me. Let's book a session and we talk about things the right way drjasonkeller@gmail.com

www.ingramcontent.com/pod-product-compliance
Lightning Source LLC
LaVergne TN
LVHW052109160826
845678LV00015B/3447

9798358387911